STRATEGIES TO MASTER CREDIT

Darnell R. McKinnon

Strategies to Master Credit, by Darnell R. McKinnon © 2019
www.mastercreditbook.com
ISBN: 978-0-578-22907-2

A NOTE FROM THE AUTHOR

I used to sit and wonder how my credit score would improve. I was having a difficult time grasping the idea of having excellent or even good credit. I would see car commercials and hear the words, "For well qualified buyers," and wonder how people were able to achieve being a well-qualified buyer. I assumed you had to be wealthy. After years of research and bumps and bruises with my personal finances, I figured it out. I decided to share the information with you. I would like to say thank you to my support system. I could not have accomplished this without support from loved ones. Anyone on this journey of restoring and improving their personal finances and credit is going to need support. There will be challenges and temptations along the way. Stay focused, stay encouraged, and stay determined.

The first step to self-improvement is knowing you need to do more.

CONTENTS

INTRODUCTION

There was a 10-year-old girl named Stacy, who sold candy to her classmates. She was very ambitious for her age. Stacy's parents owned a Sam's Club membership card, and she asked her parents if they could purchase her candy in bulk so that she could make money from selling; instead of making money from an allowance or doing chores. Her parents obliged, and purchased the candy based on the promise of Stacy maintaining good grades in school. Stacy was popular amongst her peers due to the variety of candy she sold. Her candy collection included, Skittles, Sour Patch Kids, Laffy Taffy, and Starburst.

Every day, students would line up at Stacy's desk during recess to purchase candy. Stacy sold the candy at a very reasonable rate. The Starburst were .05 cents per individual Starburst. The Skittles were .05 cents per 5 Skittles. The Sour Patch Kids and Laffy Taffy were sold in a plastic bag with both kinds of candies combined in the bag. The price for an individual bag was .50 cents.

During recess one day, a particular boy named Ren, asked Stacy if he could have a bag of candy, and pay her .50 cents back the next day. Stacy agreed and Ren paid her back the next day. He always kept his word with paying her back, so she felt comfortable with giving him a bag of candy. Ren walked away from Stacy eating candy out of the bag he received from her. During recess the next day, Ren approached Stacy with .50 cent in his hand and handed the money to Stacy. They both said, "Thank you," and then he walked away.

If Ren did not keep his word to Stacy by paying her the next day, there was a possibility she would have not let Ren walk away with the bag of candy the next time he asked. Ren built a rapport with Stacy based on his consistency with paying her back every time he received a bag of candy. The rapport Ren had with Stacy was based on the trust he built up over time by paying her back every time he received candy.

Credit works very similar to Ren and Stacy's story. The more consistent you are with paying your lender back, the better the rapport you have with your lender. Once you have a good rapport with your lender, the lender will trust you with future borrowing. Similar to if Ren skipped out on paying Stacy back; if you do the same with your lender, you will put a dent in the rapport and trust that your lender has in you; whether it's temporarily or long-term.

Before I decided to write this book, I was paying attention to all of the signs and marketing advertisements in regards to credit. Majority of the advertisement I saw was in regards to credit repair. While credit repair is a good option for people to clean up their credit, I didn't see many advertisements educating people on how to manage their credit, while restoring it on their own. The fact is, in order for you to consistently keep your credit account in good to excellent status without paying money consistently for services, you're going to have to know how to manage your credit account and personal finances.

The purpose of this book is to help people develop, grow, and maintain a good to excellent credit score on their own. The credit journey is not a short-term journey, so there's no point in thinking you can fix or grow your credit score with short-term solutions. It's going to take patience, time, dedication, effort, and genuine interest. That's right, genuine interest. See I can provide all of the tools and advice I have to offer regarding credit, but if you're not genuinely interested in taking full control of your credit and personal finances, then you won't see any results. If you're genuinely interested in taking full control over your credit, this book is for you.

CHAPTER ONE

My financial ignorance

I was born and raised in Buffalo, NY on the eastside of the city. The East Side of Buffalo has a lot of impoverished households. There are some middle-class families that live on the East Side of Buffalo, but a lot of the households are single-family households who were either raised in poverty or currently live in poverty. There is also a lack of employment in Buffalo due to many of the factories in the city being closed down over time.

When I was growing up, financial literacy was the furthest thing from my mind. My family's main interest was based on how to survive. I grew up in a single-family household, raised by my mother. I was raised along with my older sibling, Donald. We grew up poor, and while those were some of the most humbling times, a major lesson was also learned. Being poor was the norm for us. Majority of the people in our neighborhood were poor as well.

When I was in high school, the only business class my school offered was an Economics class. The class taught us about how the economy works and fluctuates, but it taught us nothing about personal finance, credit, or financial literacy. I was always interested in business and the idea of being a man who wore a suit and tie. There just seemed to be something so prestigious about a man working while being in a suit and tie. We didn't see a lot of black men wearing suits and ties in my neighborhood when I was growing up. In fact, the only time I saw black men in a suit and tie was either at church, or on television.

During my junior year of high school, college became a real possibility. Our school's guidance counselors signed us up for SATs and stayed on us about keeping our grades at a level where we would be accepted into college. Once I finally got to college, there were still no courses offered on financial literacy, personal finance, or credit.

Prior to attending college, I was always told that there will be credit card companies recruiting at college, and it was best that I stayed away from them. The reasoning I was given was credit card companies were bad. I really didn't understand why they were bad, but I decided to listen to the advice and stay away from them.

A few years after I was finished with school, I left Buffalo and relocated to Atlanta, GA. I began to understand the importance of credit and having a good credit score. I learned the phrase, "No credit is the same as bad credit," the hard way. At the time, I was dating a young lady who was more advanced in life than I was. I was trying to get on my feet and she was already established. She worked in corporate America and had both personal credit cards and company credit cards. She would often receive free hotel rooms at 4 and 5 star hotels, as well as airline flights. I thought that was cool and began to inquire about how I could get a personal credit card.

The first credit card I applied for was a credit card from a clothing department store. I was told by a couple of friends prior to applying that I may get approved for the card because I didn't have any credit and it would give me the opportunity establish credit. They were wrong. I applied and it came back that I was not approved for the store credit card. I got down on myself because I did not understand why I wasn't approved. When I received the letter in the mail that stated why I wasn't approved, it mentioned my credit history not being established enough in order to be approved. I also received a credit report in the mail as a result. The credit report had an old debt from Sprint that I had when I co-signed with my older cousin on a Sprint payment plan. Something happened where one of the phone bills wasn't paid, and the debt went to collections and ended up staying on my credit report for 7 years.

One day, I had a phone conversation with one of my friends back home in Buffalo. He was telling me that I should try to apply for a Best Buy card, because he recently had applied and was approved. I went to Best Buy the very next day and I applied for the Best Buy credit card. I was approved for a credit limit of $300. I was ecstatic leaving the Best Buy store. I used the Best Buy card to purchase electronics, CDs, and DVDs at the time. I still had no idea of how credit completely worked, and all I knew were the basics of paying back what you owed.

When I made purchases with my Best Buy card, I often maxed out my credit limit or at least tried to get as close to the limit as possible. I believed that would increase my credit score because of the amount of money I was spending. I also would let interest pile up on my Best Buy card account. Sometimes it would take me months to pay off limits of $300 or less, because I was paying the minimum limit of $25 dollars. Years down the line I've learned that's the wrong way to do it, but back then I thought there was a method to my madness. One good thing about my time with the Best Buy credit card account is I never had a late payment.

I made sure I paid all of the bills I received, even if I only paid the minimum amount.

Fast forward years down the line, I had a steady part time job. It was the type of job where you needed transportation. I had totaled out my previous car in a single vehicle car accident where I hit a tree, which shattered out majority of my windows. Luckily, I escaped that accident with no injuries. So, I needed a car and I needed one bad. My brother had an older car, but the engine was going out on the car. The car barely drove whenever you put your foot on the gas.

Knowing I needed a vehicle for work, I decided to go to car dealerships with hopes of purchasing a car. In total, I went to at least 5 dealerships. Why? All because of my credit. See, my credit wasn't what they would consider bad. It was in the mid-500s and most dealerships would work with someone in the mid-500s if they had an established credit history. My issue was I didn't have enough credit accounts or credit history. I had the one Best Buy card I received years earlier. Come to find out, that card closed a few months prior to me going to the dealership for a car because I wasn't being active with the card. The unfortunate thing about that department store card is although my utilization was bad; I never had a late payment or missed paying the bill on time every month. Letting the department store account get closed was one of the many bad credit mistakes I made.

I remember sitting in the car dealership and waiting anxiously for the car salesman to come out of the finance manager's office. They took all day calling banks and doing whatever else they could to find a bank that was willing to finance me. I remember feeling offended because the car salesman and the finance manager were in the glass office while I was out in the waiting area nervous. After about what seemed like an hour, the salesman came out and stated they were having trouble finding a bank that would give me a loan. He asked me if I knew anyone who would co-sign a car loan, so that I can get a vehicle. I told him I know people who would get approved, but they definitely wouldn't co-sign a car loan. He told me to give him a couple of days while he still looked around for loans. Being short on time, I left and went to other dealerships while getting my credit ran over and over again from attempting to get approved by a bank.

That day while going from dealership to dealership lit a fire in me. Honestly, it bruised my ego until the point I had no other choice but to come up with a game plan to change things for my personal finances and credit. Okay, I did have another choice. That choice was feeling sorry for myself and being a quitter. I decided I was tired of losing and attacked my credit problem with the small information that I learned in previous months.

Prior to getting denied for the car loans, I had been doing research on personal finances and credit. I would read any article I could find regarding credit. From there I began to gain courage about finally breaking the generational curse in my family of not understanding credit and how to establish good and excellent credit.

Once I finally stopped trying at the dealerships, over a couple of weeks span, I signed up for a Credit Karma account. When I signed up on Credit Karma, I saw that I had 26 hard inquiries with Transunion and 13 hard inquiries with Equifax. Clearly, Transunion was adding the hard inquiries as double, but that's another story. That means I was rejected for a car loan by at least 13 banks, and if not 13 different banks, it was close to it. All I knew was 13 hard inquiries was awful and 26 was awful with fire on top of it.

Having poor credit will do that to you. You're either going to get stuck in a loan with a super ridiculously high interest rate or you're going to end up with a pile of hard inquiries from dealerships attempting to get you a loan with different banks. In most cases, if credit is poor you'll end up with both scenarios. Unless you plan on paying cash for 5 and 6 figure purchases, you're going to need an established good credit score in order to get the best interest rate and control the amount of hard inquiries you receive on your credit account. I'll discuss how to do it in a later chapter.

Why read this book?

If you've begun to read this book, I'm assuming you're curious about either credit or personal finances. That's an assumption I made based on my purpose of writing this book. When I decided to write this book, I was aware that some people would be reading from a place of desperation. Maybe you applied for a home loan recently and were denied. Maybe you were denied of a job you wanted due to your credit score. Maybe you applied for an auto loan and were denied, or was approved for the loan, but at the price of a ridiculously high interest rate and length of loan. Maybe you needed a loan to pay for an emergency situation, but your financial institution denied your loan. Maybe you applied for a credit card, but were denied. Or, maybe you just want to have a good credit score and get more out of your financial situation.

Whatever is your reason for reading this book, I want you to know this book was not written to provide quick credit solutions. In a world where there are quick credit fixes available, this book hardly provides any of them. You're going to need to know how to manage your credit portfolio for the rest of your life, even well after you hit the credit score of your dreams. Sure, you can hire a credit repair company, but if you don't know how to manage your credit portfolio you more than likely will need those services again in the future. That's more money out of your pocket in the future towards something you can do on your own.

This book is about breaking and developing new habits. It is about using strategies provided that not only helps your credit score in the present, but well into the future. This book provides long-term credit solutions. So before you continue reading, ask yourself why are you reading this book? Whatever your current score is, you can benefit from reading this book. If your credit score is poor, this book has the tools to help you get your credit score to excellent. If your credit score is fair, this book has the same tools it has for people with poor credit. If your credit is good or excellent, there is information in this book that can help you maintain, improve your score, and master your credit.

I decided to write this book for anyone who is interested in growing, developing, and maintaining their credit score. That should literally be everyone on the planet. The average American doesn't have money saved up in order to make big purchases flat out. One thing you will read multiple times throughout this book is that you should never underestimate the power of credit. You never know when you will need to use your credit. Once you're done reading this book, you will be equipped with the information and tools it takes in order to develop, grow, and maintain your credit portfolio, but your success with doing so all depends on one person: You.

You may be one of the people reading this and probably thinking why read this book when you can go and purchase a trade line that will raise your credit score by large points almost instantly. Guess what? You can. But think about this. What happens when you achieve good or excellent credit through a trade line, but you still don't know how to manage debt or maintain your credit profile, which results in your credit score crashing? Are you going to pay for more trade lines? What happens if the person who owns the account that you're authorized on unfortunately has to close the account and your credit score crashes? Are you going to pay for another trade line? If you're fine with constantly spending hundreds or thousands of dollars to bail you out of a problem you can solve on your own, then go right ahead.

One thing I would like you to keep in mind is this book is based on future results more than results in the present. Why is this book more future based? Because the practice of maintaining good or excellent credit is for future purposes and future needs. Sure, you'll benefit from the information in this book in the present. In fact, some of you may see positive results in your credit score in the span of a couple months if you apply all of the information provided in this book. However, what happens once you receive everything that good credit can get you?

If you get approved for the vehicle loan on the vehicle you desire, are you going to stop trying to maintain your credit score? Once you get approved for the home loan on the home you desire, will you behave as if you no longer need your good credit anymore? One thing I've learned in life is the more you receive, the more you usually desire. Good credit gives you the ability to continue to leverage your credit even after you've acquired the things you desired when you initially needed credit.

Long after the car that you purchased depreciates in value, you're going to more than likely want to purchase another vehicle to replace it. What if you don't have the savings to purchase one flat out with cash? You're going to need your credit score in order to receive a good loan. Wouldn't you like to know that you're credit score is more than good enough to receive the lowest interest rate possible on your next vehicle loan? Wouldn't you like to know your chances of getting approved for another home loan in the future if needed? What about emergencies and other financial needs if you don't have the cash to back you up? Your credit profile becomes your life vest, especially if you don't have the cash. Having a good credit score is the difference between being rescued in freezing waters by a boat and floating in the freezing waters with a life vest. Paying high interest rates is basically giving away free money over time. I'm sure you can think of other places you would rather place those hundreds or thousands of dollars instead of giving it to a financial institution because they approved you for a loan with a high interest rate due to your poor or fair credit.

I decided to write this book because I believe achieving a good credit score is simple. When I first began the journey to better my credit, I viewed it as a huge mountain that I would have to climb. The more I dove into the information and applied what I learned; I soon realized that having good and excellent credit is very achievable. The only person who can prevent you from improving your credit score and portfolio is you. Your participation is needed as much as the information that I'm providing in this book. You could have paid hundreds or sometimes thousands of dollars and went the credit repair route, but something deep inside of you sparked your curiosity to realize that maybe you too can improve your credit score as well, on your own. You were right.

CHAPTER TWO

Take a dose of discipline and patience

I don't have anything against credit repair companies. Anyone who is helping people turn their credit around for the better is all right with me. However, I believe that establishing and maintaining good credit is less about what someone can do for you and more about what you can do for yourself. Good habits regarding financial responsibility are something that should be made habitual during this process. I believe in individuals improving and maintaining their credit on their own because of what they'll learn along the way. The credit journey is similar to the old proverb, "Give a man a fish and you feed him for a day; teach a man to fish and you feed him for a lifetime." I view credit and financial literacy in the same way. You're about to learn how to fish.

Maintaining a healthy credit score is a skill. Regardless of how many people may believe that it's not, it's actually a skill. I consider it a skill and talent that takes a couple years to firmly develop. Think of professional athletes, they didn't just become professional athletes overnight without developing and mastering their skills. It took years for them to develop their talent, then improve (grow) their talent, and last but not least, maintain their talent. They put in hours working on their skills. They sacrificed a lot of time out of their social lives in order to get their skills to the professional level. I've heard stories of professional athletes waking up at 4am and 5am in order to work on their conditioning and skills. The same applies to developing, growing, and maintaining credit, minus the physical part. However, the same amount of mental discipline and dedication needs to be applied in order to achieve the best results. You literally need to become obsessed with credit, and I have a feeling after you see the positive results of your credit score rising, you will become obsessed with it.

The truth is it's going to take some time for your credit score to improve, especially if your credit score is currently in the poor or fair range. It is very important to get out of the mentality of wanting your credit to improve instantly. I believe that instant gratification in the form of personal finance is a disaster waiting to happen. Sure your score may temporarily improve, but if you don't learn the skills of growing and maintaining your credit, you'll eventually go back to having poor or fair credit. There are ways your credit score can improve drastically in a short period of time, such as trade line accounts, and getting old invalid or unverified collection accounts removed from your credit bureau accounts. However, the focus of this book is to teach you the good independent building blocks with financial literacy and credit.

It took me 4 years to go from a 549 credit score to an excellent credit score. It didn't just happen over a span of a couple of months. Was it tough at times when my score didn't budge? Of course it was. However, there's beauty in the process of improving and maintaining your credit. No one else can take credit for your credit score once you've improved it to the good or excellent credit range on your own. I've learned more from managing my own credit than I've learned from reading any book or article related to credit. I decided to share what I've learned from managing my credit over the years as well as consulting other people with theirs. I know this book will assist you with managing your own credit in the present and the future.

Think of your credit as a crop. When farmers are growing crop they realize not only do they need to practice patience in order to harvest, there are also steps they take to maintain and grow the crops until it's time to harvest them. You have to think long-term in reference to your credit. Patience is the first step that anyone who is working towards improving his or her credit needs to complete. Without practicing patience, it will be very hard to break bad money habits and get the best results from this book.

Dealing with the discouragement

I remember back to when I first applied for my secured credit cards. The excitement I felt was similar to the feeling of graduating from school. I knew the decision I made to get those two secured cards would change my financial future. I also knew that it would have my credit score reach levels that it never reached before. But what I didn't know was my patience was going to be tested over and over again throughout the whole process.

When my score finally rose into the mid-600s, it stayed there for at least 7 months. I was at a 660 credit score for 4 months and it became so discouraging. I honestly wanted to stop the credit process and give up. The score would not move at all. I started to believe there was no way the credit process worked past a 660 credit score. I even contacted a couple of consultants asking them why my score was staying the same.

They didn't have an answer for me. I was making my payments on time, keeping my utilization low, and not applying for any new credit, but my score still would not move.

I became discouraged. However, I finally realized eventually the score would rise and it wouldn't stay the same forever. I put on my patience hard hat and let the months go by, while being consistent with my utilization, on-time payments, and not applying for any new credit. Then one day the score finally went up a couple of points. It was a relief, and at that moment I learned that a combination of patience and consistency are needed in order to develop, grow, and maintain a good credit score. After it went up those couple of points, my score continued to rise drastically over the next span of months by applying the credit factors you'll learn throughout this book.

Even when my credit reached the excellent credit range I experienced more discouragement. My score would go up and down every month while in the excellent credit range. It even dropped into the good credit range a couple of times. I didn't make any changes and continued with my consistency, but the score was still jumping all over the place. I know that's nothing to stress over, but that's just an example of credit for you. The numbers will go up and down and sometimes stay the same for months, even if you're doing everything you're supposed to be doing consistently. If you get too caught up in the numbers it can discourage you and if you're not consistent and determined enough, the discouragement will force you to give up on your skill of developing, growing, and maintaining your good credit. Don't let discouragement stop you. Stay consistent and focused on the task at hand, not the number of your score.

The one thing I would like you to use as your motivating factor is the thing or things you plan on doing with your good credit score. You're going to get discouraged during this journey. It's not a short journey, but instead a life journey. Your credit will need to be managed over the period of your whole life and adulthood, so discouragements are going to come. You may go through a rough financial patch down the line that causes your credit score to drop, but the one thing you'll know how to do after reading this book is bounce back. This is why it is important for you to view discouragement as a part of the process and not a boulder in the road you're on during your credit journey.

Avoid desperation

One major way people get themselves in a financial bind is through desperation. Maybe their engine or transmission went on an old car and they didn't have enough money saved up to purchase another one in full, so they had to finance another vehicle. Maybe they had a family emergency and they needed to fly out of town, but in order to do so they had to purchase their hotel room and plane ticket with a credit card because they didn't have the money saved up. Maybe they needed a personal loan, because they didn't have the savings to cover the expense that was needed.

The key thing I'm mentioning is not having the money saved up. Most people view credit as the savior when you don't have the financial savings. This book is not about bailing yourself out so that you can avoid good money management and savings skills. This book is about teaching you how to be financially responsible with managing your debt. There's no bail out. The safest bail is keeping your own self out of financial trouble. Yes, unfortunate events happen to all of us at some point in time. There are times when we need to spend more money than what we have in savings. However, you still need to have a financial plan or some form of insurance or security just in case unfortunate things do happen. Even when you're done with this book and apply everything you've learned, it doesn't mean you should stop practicing good personal finance skills. This book is about building good personal finance skills in the form of credit.

One important personal finance skill you need to develop is planning ahead with savings and your money management. Good and excellent credit helps you avoid being desperate. The ironic thing is you can't maintain good or excellent credit if you're desperate. Developing, growing, and maintaining your credit and avoiding desperation work together simultaneously. By the end of this book, you'll understand why desperation in the financial world often damages your credit.

CHAPTER THREE

The concept of credit

I'm sure everyone who comes across this book and reads it are from different financial backgrounds. I come from a financial background where financial literacy was close to non-existent. In my younger days, it seemed like acquiring enough money to keep my head above water was nearly impossible. I spent more than half of my life in school and not one time did I receive a lecture or lesson in school regarding the importance of credit. I don't know if they had classes on credit in other schools, but the schools I attended did not teach about credit. We learned about Economics, Accounting, Business management, and even Business Finance. We never had one lesson on personal finance or credit.

I find it interesting because credit and personal finances are two of the most important financial aspects of adulthood, yet there were not many classes or courses in schools regarding credit or personal finances. The truth is the World and financial institutions thrive on debt. The whole concept of credit is based on how well you manage your financial debt. Without debt, your credit score will suffer and without credit, there's a chance your financial status will suffer unless you're someone with a surplus of available cash or assets.

The U.S. recession that took place in 2008 was a result of banks' lending to too many people who were not qualified for home loans. It was referred to as the Subprime mortgage crises. The banks were approving and lending to homeowners who either had credit scores that were too low to be homeowners, and borrowers who could not financially afford the homes they were approved to purchase. The banks were eventually bailed out of the crises, but the effects of the subprime mortgage crises still linger today.

The reason why the effects of the subprime mortgage crises still linger is not because the banks are not able to approve homeowners for loans. The effects come from history currently repeating itself in the present with subprime mortgage loans currently being given out to borrowers. People who cannot afford home loans or loans in general are still being approved for loans. The loans are manipulated in ways that make the borrower believe they can afford the full terms of the loans, but in reality their starting off their loans upside down in debt and paying their early payments majority towards interest. The same applies to people with bad or poor credit. If your credit is poor and you don't have the finances to purchase whatever you need a loan for flat out, then you cannot afford it. However, since banks and other financial institutions thrive on making more money, they don't see it that way.

There are some financial experts and advisors who don't approve of the concept behind credit. They view credit as something that's bad and evil. Judging by the way a lot of people dig themselves in deep financial holes with subprime loans, high interest rate vehicle notes, and maxing out credit cards, I understand their opinion. However, I believe credit is vital and very important. The average person needs credit in order to obtain things such as a durable vehicle or a home to live in. Everyone is not in the financial position to purchase a vehicle or buy a home with cash, and that's where credit comes into play.

There is information regarding credit just about everywhere. There are videos on the Internet, commercials on televisions, infomercials on the radio, forums, blogs, as well as books written regarding credit. The main reason why I decided to write this book is because even though there's a plethora of information out in the world regarding credit, a lot of people still don't understand how to develop, grow, and maintain a good or excellent credit score.

Credit is based on borrowing. Similar to the story at the beginning of this book, if you borrow you have to pay back. Some people struggle with the concept of credit. They view credit as a tool used as a rope to pull them out of a financial hole. However, credit is based on how well a borrower pays back a lender. The only time a financial hole is created is when the borrower doesn't play by the rules of the lender. I view credit as a chess piece in a game that many people don't want to play, but often times is forced to play. Anyone who's a responsible and determined human being can develop, grow, and maintain their credit. I'll provide you with the tools in this book.

I personally believe a good credit score is attainable for everyone. No matter your current circumstance, the one key factor when it comes to improving your credit is patience. You will see the word patience plenty of times throughout this book. You may even be tired of seeing the word by the time you finish reading the last sentence of this book. Reading this book from start to finish is your first test of patience. There is something in every chapter that you can benefit from if applied to your personal finances.

Good debt vs Bad debt

The people who are big believers in being totally debt free will probably not like what I'm about to say. I'm a believer in paying down as much bad debt as possible and being on the road to financial freedom. However, I'm what many people who believe in being totally debt free would consider a hypocrite because I also believe in having good standing credit accounts and chopping down bad debt simultaneously. For some reason, people believe you cannot do both. Some people feel if you have good or excellent credit you can't have financial freedom and there are others who believe if you want financial freedom you can't have any debt.

Everyone who's reading this book is not in the financial situation to pay down their financial debt in lump sums immediately. It's not like people who can make large sums of payments straight cash. This is where understanding the concept of paying off and managing your debt comes into play. Through the process of you paying off all of your bad debt, you'll in return help build your credit up to a point where it will be good even without any debt. Let's be realistic, this world thrives on debt. I view debt similar to how a lot of nutritionists view carbs. There are good carbs and bad carbs. I haven't come across a nutritionist that would prefer their clients to not consume any carbs at all.

The same applies to good debt vs. bad debt. There may be a time in your future where large sums of money are not available in a short period as it was when you paid down all of your debt. What happens if an emergency pops up or you need to a large sum of money immediately for something? If that happens, you'll more than likely need a loan of some type. Having good or excellent credit provides you with the option of being able to take out that loan at a good interest rate. If your goal is to have no debt at all, then this book is probably not for you. This book is about learning how to manage your good debt in a way that will benefit you in the present as well in the future, through your credit score.

Everyone has their own definition about what they consider to be good debt and what they consider bad debt. I believe good debt is any debt in relation to an item that can give you positive financial leverage. Positive financial leverage means getting more in return than your initial investment. A home would be something that I consider to be good debt. There are some people who consider a home as bad debt because they feel that you're better off paying month to month for an apartment. Some people also believe in paying a home off with cash. However, the average person more than likely cannot purchase a livable home with cash. That's where a home loan comes into play. A home is something that can be either passed down to future generations of your family, or sold for more than the price you purchased it for. Also, a business that has a good customer or client base is also something I would consider to be good debt. Although, there is no guarantee that a business will work out, so whether or not a business is good or bad debt is subjective. Smart investments of things that don't depreciate with time are things I consider to be good debt.

The things I consider bad debt are any debts that either depreciates with time or don't provide more of a return for you in the future. I'll assume most financial experts consider credit cards to be bad debt. I'll assume they believe credit cards are bad debt because they carry interest. However, if you read this book in its entirety you will never view credit cards the same anymore. There are ways to avoid interest with credit cards and those ways will be explained later on. Collections and student loans are also considered bad debt. A vehicle loan or any personal loan that was used to purchase something that depreciates is considered bad debt. Tax liens were also considered bad debt, but they were recently removed from credit reports by the 3 major credit bureaus in 2018.

Something to think about as you continue reading is the way you view debt. Your ability to manage your debt is what will make or break your credit score. It is very important for you to understand how debt works and why the credit bureaus value your management of debt so much. The goal should be to at least get your debt to a status where it is current and in good standing.

THE 5 CREDIT CATEGORIES THAT MAKE UP YOUR CREDIT SCORE

Your credit score is made up of 5 categories. Those categories are: payment history, the amount owed, length of credit history, new credit accounts, and the type of credit accounts. These 5 categories combined together make up 100% of your credit score. The goal is for you to have master knowledge in all 5 of these categories by the time you're done reading this book. All of these categories need to work in unison in order for you to obtain excellent credit. If you have difficulty managing one of these 5 credit categories, it will result in you losing points on your credit score. If you slack with one category, it will have a domino effect with the other categories. All of these categories are very important when developing, growing, and maintaining credit. Do not view a category as unimportant because the percentage it contributes to your credit score is smaller than the other categories. Through years of experience, all of these categories work together. You too will realize they all work together, and you can make positive adjustments with each category that works best for your own credit profile.

Remember, everyone's credit profile is different. Some people may have more accounts in one category than others. One thing remains the same no matter if your credit profile is short or long, or new or old; you have to work all of these categories simultaneously in order to get the best results with your credit score. I'm going to share very important information on how these 5 categories contribute to your score.

Payment history 35%

Your payment history contributes for 35% of your credit score. Payment history is the highest percentage category out of all of the categories that go into the bureaus deciding your credit score. Payment history is based on how well you pay your balances every month. If you never miss any payments any of your credit accounts, you'll have a payment history of 100%. If you miss any payments or if you're late with making payments, it will hurt your payment history for and as a result will hurt your credit score overall. It is very important you pay your credit accounts on time every month. If you have to set up a monthly automatic payment for each account you have, do it. Develop a habit of paying all of your accounts on time. The words "late payment" need to become foreign to you in order for you to have success with your credit.

Amount owed 30%

Next is the amount you owe. A popular word to describe the amount you owe is debt. Your debt contributes to 30% of your credit score. I'm assuming everyone reading this book knows what debt is. To break it down in laymen's term, it's basically the amount you owe from the amount you borrowed. If you borrowed $60 dollars, but you only paid back $30, then your debt is the $30 that's left over. It's easy math in regards to the break down. Where it gets tricky for some people is most of the time in the financial world, the amount borrowed comes with interest. One way to avoid paying interest on accounts that are not installment accounts is to avoid late payments and avoid carrying balances over to the next month. I'll touch more on that later in this book.

So far we are at 65% in regards to categories contributing to your credit score. That means your payment history and debt makes up majority of your credit score. Payment history and the amount you owe go together like peanut butter and jelly. Those two factors are very important and I'm sure most people are already aware of the impact those two factors have regarding their credit score. However, a lot of people lose points on their credit score by not balancing and maintaining the other 3 major categories of their credit score. When doing simple math, those 3 other categories contribute to 35% of your credit score. So, if you're doing well with your payment history and paying off your debt but yet your score is still stagnant, you're more than likely not doing a good job of managing the 3 other categories that contribute to your credit score.

Length of Credit history 15%

Length of credit history contributes to 15% of your credit score. It is my belief that your credit history is just as important to your credit score as payment history and the amount owed are. Let's say you're 30 years old and back when you were 20 years old you opened up a credit card account with a department store. That would mean you have 10 years of credit history for that account. If you have a good payment history with that account, it would contribute to your credit score in a positive way. I would advise you to never close an old credit card account even if you don't use the card anymore. Attempt to make small purchases that are easy to pay off such as a pair of socks or something even cheaper, in order to keep the account open. Closing down an old account will hurt your length of credit history, and as a result it will hurt your credit score. Opening recent accounts can also potentially hurt your credit score. The more recent the account you open, it lowers the overall years on your length of credit history. If you just opened up an account recently, it could possibly contribute to your credit account in a negative way, short term. Recent accounts tie into the next category.

New credit 10%

New credit is basically any credit account you open recently. If you go out and finance a vehicle, it will count as new credit. If you get a new credit card or loan, it will count as new credit. Even things such as student loans count as new credit if you received one in recent history. New credit impacts your score short term. With credit, the longer and healthier your credit accounts, the more points you will have on your credit score. New credit goes hand in hand with credit inquiries. There are two types of inquiries. There are soft inquiries, which are harmless to your credit score. Sites such as Credit Karma, credit card company advertisers, as well as other free online credit services often use soft inquiries. Soft inquiries are known in the credit world as soft pulls. The other inquiry is known as a hard inquiry. Hard inquiries impact your credit in a negative way, and I'll touch more on hard inquiries in a later chapter in this book in order to give you a complete understanding of how they affect your score. With new credit inquiries, it is very important for you to keep your hard inquiries under 2 per credit bureau per every 2-year period in order for it not to have a major impact on your credit score. That means, if you have 1 hard inquiry with Transunion, 2 hard inquiries with Equifax, and 2 hard inquiries with Experian, do not apply for credit with any credit institution that pulls credit from either Equifax or Experian. I will have a full section on this further into the book where I fully break this down.

Types of credit used 10%

The last category of the 5 major categories that affect your credit score is the type of credit you use. There are two main types of credit used. You have installment loans, which are loans that are based on you paying off the amount you've borrowed over a certain time frame. There are also loans such as credit card accounts, and sometimes utilities. It is good to have at least one of each type of loan in order to help your credit score. That means if you only have credit card accounts on your credit report, it would benefit you to have an installment account on your credit report as well, if you can afford it. Paying off a credit card balance and an installment loan on a month-to-month basis pleases the credit scoring system. Installment accounts can be student loans, mortgages, car loans, and personal loans. The credit bureaus like to see you with both installment accounts and credit accounts. Remember their whole scoring system is based on debt and how well you can manage and pay debt off.

If you merge all 5 categories together simultaneously they make up your credit score. If you're struggling with managing one category, it will affect another category. They all work hand in hand together. Your payment history over a period of time cuts down on the amount of debt you owe. Your length of credit history works with your payment history, because if you miss too many payments a financial institution will more than likely close your account and sell it to a collection agency, which will in return affect the amount you owe, and your payment history. Your new credit accounts contribute to your length of credit history. The newer the credit account, the greater the risk for it to affect your score in a negative way. The types of credit you have works with all of the other 4 categories, because if you mismanaged any of the other 4 categories it can potentially lead to closed accounts which will affect the amount of accounts on your credit report, which in return will affect the type of credit you use. Remember, adding all 5 categories together make up 100% of your credit score. Managing all 5 categories on a month-to-month basis will work wonders for your score.

CHAPTER FOUR

The Credit Process

Think of your credit score as a big pot of Gumbo. There are all different types of ingredients in Gumbo that makes it the dish that it is. In this case, you're the chef who's attempting to make the best pot of gumbo as possible. When it comes to your credit profile, you have to be willing to do things simultaneously in order to achieve the best possible credit score. Some people believe credit is as simple as paying off your bills every month, but unfortunately the way your credit score is determined is much more complicated than that.

There are certain techniques you have to follow on a month-to-month basis in order for your credit score to consistently trend upwards. Not following these techniques on a month-to-month basis may very well likely have a negative effect on your credit score. Some people may think that's not big of a deal, because you can just correct the mistakes the next month and your score will increase. However, I want you to keep in mind that you never know when you will need to leverage your credit score. It is always important to try to keep your credit score trending upwards until it gets to the point where it can't go any higher. At that point you still have a job to do, and that job is maintaining your score and credit profile.

In this chapter I'm going to discuss the many techniques you should use to grow and maintain your credit score. Remember, these techniques should all be used simultaneously and on a month-to-month basis. If you follow these techniques, your score will be trending upwards in no type. You have to do them all simultaneously in order to get the best results.

The credit card rule

There's a credit card rule that made my credit soar. After I had a fire lit in me from so many loan application rejections I decided it was time I swallow my pride and sign up for a Secured credit card account. I had been doing research for weeks via the Internet on ways to get a credit card while having bad or established credit.

One day I stumbled across an article about Discover bank having a new secured credit card. It was around the time period when Discover didn't promote its secured card on their website. I read about how the card had no annual fee and how it was a good starter card for people who were trying to establish and build their credit. I decided to go to Discover.com and speak with one of their customer service representatives regarding the Discover It secured card. The representative told me that I would have to apply for their regular credit card first. I applied for their regular credit card and was denied. Then I received an invite to apply for the Discover It secured card. I applied and I was instantly approved. They sent me an email telling me I had a certain time frame to pay my deposit with a minimum credit limit starting at $200. My next pay period, I paid $300 and received my Discover secured credit card in the mail a week or so later.

Receiving a secured card in the mail was one of the best feelings I've ever felt. For the first time, I was able to have a credit card that wasn't a store credit card. I also was eligible to receive some of the same rewards that unsecured Discover credit card member received. The good thing about the Discover It secured card back then was the bank reported my account to Experian, Transunion, and Equifax as a secured card. Even better, a couple of weeks after receiving my Discover card, I received a special offer in the mail from my bank to apply for their secured credit card. It helped that the deposit needed for my bank's secured card was only $300 minimum in order to receive a credit limit of $500.

Once I received my card, I instantly began to apply the credit card rule based on all of the knowledge I gained from reading about credit. I thought back to my Best Buy card and how I didn't receive a big jump in my credit score, as I would have liked. The reason was because I was using the card as if it were my own money. The credit limit was $300 and I would make a purchase with the card for $297. I figured as long as I paid back the minimum amount required every month and avoid late fees; I would be good. I didn't care about the amount of interest my card account was building up monthly because I believed that's what it was supposed to do. That is not the way you should use a credit card. If you believe that's the way to use a credit card you'll never achieve good or excellent credit.

The credit card rule is to not spend money that you know you cannot pay off in full the next month. To take it a step further, the rule also applies to the amount you can spend every month. You literally have to give yourself an allowance every month in order for this to work. Those are two major credit card rules that must be followed in order to get into the good and excellent credit range. One big mistake a lot of people tend to make is using their credit card in order to dig themselves out of financial holes. If you're an emotional spender and you don't have the finances in your bank account or saved somewhere to finance your emotional spending, please do not use your credit card(s) and go above the utilization this book suggest you stay under. If you do, you risk putting yourself in deep debt, which in return will damage your credit for the present and the long run.

Your credit limit is not your money

You may be reading this book with the same mentality I used to have regarding credit. You may believe cash is king and credit cards are dangerous. I'm fine with you believing those things, because I used to have the same mentality as well. You're not completely wrong or right if you believe either of those two things. Cash is king in instances where you can financially afford to pay for things with your own money without creating financially hardships. Credit cards are dangerous if you do not know how to use them to your advantage. You'll create debt you cannot manage and put yourself in a financial hole. However, everyone cannot afford to pay out of pocket for things such as a home or a car, so therefore they need a good credit score in order to receive a lower interest rate from the bank and good loan amount.

The reason I decided to write this book was to spark the thought of viewing credit different. Credit is not something you should view as being dangerous. My goal is for you to finish reading the last chapter of this book and understand credit is not dangerous and you could use it to your advantage if you want to. I want you to finish reading this book and be motivated while viewing credit as leverage in the financial world and nothing more.

Some people will probably read what I just stated and think it's bogus. They may view credit as a life vest that basically provides free money that's available to them. They probably believe money from a loan or credit card account is there to bail them out if they ever fall on hard times or need emergency spending. Some people view credit as part of their income. They probably believe credit is extra money they can use to splurge on expensive vacations or go shopping for the Holidays and other special occasions. I know some people personally who share the same ideology as the previous mentioned.

However, credit is a tool. It is one of the most powerful tools in the financial world if used correctly. Credit, along with determination can turn someone with below average income into a millionaire. Good credit is a leverage tool. It can open up many financial doors for you if you leverage your credit correctly.

There's a famous video clip of former NY Jets head coach Herman Edwards. During a postgame interview, Edwards stated the famous quote, "You play to win the game." That's my response to anyone who has doubts about creating debt in order to enhance your credit score. I'll admit I don't like debt at all. However, I know debt is needed in order to establish, build, and maintain a healthy credit score. There's a method to debt though.

There are a lot of people with the ideology of not having any debt and being debt free. Others have the ideology of having debt in order to create financial leverage and provide the opportunity to get loans for assets such as homes and investment properties. I take both of their ideologies and combine them together. There is a way to be debt free and still have good credit. It's done through patience and financial discipline.

Part of that discipline is the understanding that the credit limit on your credit card account is nothing more than a chess piece. The money on your credit account, whether loan or credit limit is not your money. Do not carry the mentality of believing that your credit account has your money in it. It doesn't. The money belongs to the bank or credit union that issued you the credit card or loan. When people believe the money in their credit limit is their money, they risk creating debt they cannot afford to pay off. Never view the money in any of your credit accounts as being your own money.

Credit Utilization

As I stated previously, I began to research as much information as possible regarding ways to manage my credit limit. That's when I learned about credit utilization. Credit utilization simply is the percentage of your credit limit that you use. If you have a credit limit of $1,000 and you decide to spend $1,000, your credit card's utilization is 100%. Never, and I mean never have 100% utilization on a credit account. You may think you're doing yourself a favor if you pay the $1,000 balance off the very next month, but your high utilization will cause your credit score to drop, even though you've paid off your balance the next month. The credit bureaus hate seeing high utilization on credit card accounts. It has all of the signals of a credit risk.

Common knowledge in the world of personal finance is for credit card users to keep their card utilization under 30%. That means if you have a credit limit of $1,000, you don't want to spend more than $300. That's a decent utilization, however we are about "playing to win the game." What worked for myself, and plenty of other people I've consulted, is keeping your utilization under 10%. So yes, that means even if you only have a credit limit of $200 such as I did with my Discover It secured card, never spend more than $20. You may think if you're going to spend so little money there is no point in having a credit card. Always remember your credit card limit is not your money, it's a tool. The tool is a chess piece to assist you with winning. If you have to use a calculator in order for this to work best for yourself then do it. If your credit limit is $345 then you want to multiply that amount by .10. That number will let you know the maximum amount you can spend with that credit card each month, until you receive a credit limit increase.

The goal is to develop financial discipline through wise spending habits. Yes, only spending 10% of your credit limit can be annoying especially when you get the urge to shop or purchase things. If you do get that urge, use your own cash instead. The money on your credit card account is not free money.

View your 10% utilization as a one-month loan. Do not let your credit card account gain interest. When I first started applying for credit cards after my two secured cards graduated, I didn't worry about what the card's APR was because I planned on either using my card similar to a charge account or not using the card at all.

A charge credit card account is a card that you have to pay off every month. Charge cards are usually offered through American Express. If you do not pay off the amount you charged, there's a strong possibility your account will get cancelled. The reason why I view credit cards the same as charge accounts goes back to the ideology that the money in your credit account is not your money. If someone loans you money, you usually pay them back in a certain time frame. The payback time frame for you should be every time you receive your credit card account bill.

Do not skip a month paying your bill, no matter how much you owe. Another reason why you should only set your credit utilization to 10% or less is so you don't have to pay back large amounts of money when your bill is due. Paying off your bill every month will be much easier to do when you only spent 10% or less of your credit limit. This will not only help you not overspend monthly on your credit cards, it will also help you develop discipline and create a habit of paying off whatever you spend.

Your credit card balance

Your credit card balance ties into your credit account's utilization with the 3 credit Bureaus. Think of your credit card balance as food and your utilization as working out. I don't know about you, but for me working out on a full stomach is very hard to do. I don't have productive workouts when I work out on a full stomach. However, when I eat just the right amount of food to give me energy during my workout, I have a pretty good work out.

The same applies with your credit card balance and how it affects your credit utilization. When you keep your utilization under 10%, it helps your credit utilization on your credit score every month. One cool thing about keeping your utilization low is it makes your balance easier to pay off. The key to developing, growing, and maintaining good credit is to pay off what you spend every month. I know some people prefer to just pay the minimum balance on their bill every month, however that method does not impress the credit scoring system like paying off your balance every month.

I always tell the people I help with credit to think of their credit card or account balance as a one-month loan. That's basically what it is. It's a one-month loan from the bank or credit card Company to prove to them that you can manage your debt and pay back what you spend in a timely manner. Remember the story in the beginning of the book about the girl selling candy? The same applies to this method. You pay what you spend.

If you go out to the store and spend $100, you need to pay back the full $100 once you receive your bill and before the bill's due date. I prefer my clients to pay their bill at least 5 days before the due date if they can, so that their payment clears on time and there won't be any issues. If you can't pay 5 days prior to your bill's due date; at least try to pay 2 days before the due date.

I cannot stress to you any stronger how important paying off your balance every month is. Paying off your balance means paying your statement balance in full every month. You may ask, "What if I spent $1,000 the prior month?" My answer is, you shouldn't spend what you cannot afford to pay off the next month. As I stated in the earlier chapter, your credit card's credit limit is not your money. It's nothing but a one-month loan that you have to pay back the next month. Spending large amounts on your credit card or having bad spending habits only hurt your ability to pay the money back the next month. If you don't have a high enough credit limit on your card, spending large amounts of money on your credit card could not only hurt your credit utilization but it can also hurt your personal finances.

This book is about creating positive habits in reference to your credit. Keeping your utilization low and your balance paid off every month creates good habits. Not only will you become better with spending money, you'll also develop a habit of budgeting to fit certain monthly expenses into your utilization. Always remember, keeping your balance low and paying it off monthly is just as important as not getting any new delinquent accounts.

No such thing as Interest for you

When you get approved for a credit card the financial lender usually lets you know your APR (annual percentage rate). It's the amount of interest you're charged over a 12-month period. For people with great credit, their interest rate may be in the teen numbers. For others, the interest rate will more than likely be in the 20% range depending on the financial institution you received your credit card from.

When you receive your first billing statement, you'll notice a required minimum payment. When developing, growing, and maintaining your credit score, the APR and minimum payment requirement need to be non-existent to you. Why do they both need to be non-existent? Because you will treat your credit card exactly like a charge card. A charge card is a card that's similar to a credit card, but you have to pay the balance off every month. Recently, American Express created a pay over-time feature for their charge cards where you can pay your balance over a time period. There is an APR and minimum payment required for it. However, as stated, those two things are irrelevant because when developing, growing, and maintaining your credit, you need to pay your balance off every month, no matter how much you've charged to your card.

If you go out to the store and spend $100, you need to pay back the full $100 once you receive your bill and before the bill's due date. Always pay your statement balance. I prefer my clients to pay their bill at least 5 days before the due date if they can, so that their payment clears on time and there won't be any issues. If you can't pay 5 days prior to your bill's due date; at least try to pay 2 days before the due date.

I cannot stress to you any stronger how important paying off your balance every month is. You may ask, "What if I spent $1,000 the prior month?" My answer is, you shouldn't spend what you cannot afford to pay off the next month. As I stated in the earlier chapter, your credit card's credit limit is not your money. It's nothing but a one-month loan that you have to pay back in full the next month. Spending large amounts on your credit card or having bad spending habits only hurt your ability to pay the money back the next month. If you don't have a high enough credit limit on your card, spending large amounts of money on your credit card could not only hurt your credit utilization, but it can also hurt your personal finances. Be wise when using your credit cards to purchase things. If you know you'll have a hard time paying the money you spend back the next month, you should not make the purchase or you can use cash or a debit card to make the purchase. This whole credit process is about discipline and your ability to be responsible enough to manage your debt.

This book is about creating positive habits in reference to your credit. Keeping your utilization low and your balance paid off every month creates good habits. Not only will you become better and more mindful when spending money, you'll also develop a habit of budgeting to fit certain monthly expenses into your utilization. Always remember, keeping your balance low and paying it off monthly is just as important as not getting any new delinquent accounts.

Avoid new delinquencies

This is a tricky chapter in this book. Unless you're wealthy, we all go through rough financial patches at least once in our lives. You may lose your job; have to miss work due to sickness or injury, go through hard times with your business, or have trouble acquiring a full time job that provides health benefits. I don't think anyone can look down on people who are going through hard times due to any of the previous mentioned dilemmas.

I remember when my credit was poor. I had delinquencies on my credit account. I think at one time I had a total of 6 medical delinquencies on my credit account. Those delinquencies came from emergency room visits during times when I was going through financial hardships and didn't have medical or dental insurance. I wasn't aware of urgent care during those times, nor was I aware that for me urgent care would have been the best option instead of the ER.

As time goes by, I learned the best option was urgent care due to it being affordable for people who may have income, but don't have health insurance. Now of course, if you have a serious medical emergency the ER is the best option. However, if you do not have a serious medical emergency, urgent care might be the best option in order to keep the cost down. I am not a nurse or medical professional, so determining whether or not your medical emergency is for you and a medical professional to determine.

If you do have the misfortune where you have to go to urgent care or the ER, ask if you can arrange monthly payment arrangements if you can't afford to pay the full amount on the day of your visit. Completely ignoring the bill is how you end up with medical debt in collections. Having medical debt in collections not only hurts your score, but the debt is also hard to get removed depending on how new the debt is.

Another type delinquency you want to avoid are delinquencies from utility bills. While developing, growing, and maintaining your credit, you want to make sure you always pay your utility bills on time. Whichever utilities you have, make sure you pay them on time every month. The last thing you want is the utility company reporting your delinquency to the credit bureaus. It will hurt your score.

I remember I used to have a Sprint phone while I was in college. I didn't have much knowledge about credit back then, so I wasn't worried about whether or not my phone account affected my credit. I remember I decided to switch over to a phone company called Cricket. However, when I left Sprint I had a balance due. I didn't pay the balance on the Sprint account and the balance ended up going into collections. Of course, I wasn't even aware that the Sprint account was on my credit account until years down the line when I applied for the Best Buy card and received a free credit report.

Paying your utilities off once you close any account is important. Do your due diligence when you decide to part ways with a utility or phone company. Double check and make sure you leave that company with a zero balance, and make sure you get it put in writing via a statement. It is very important to not carry old debt that you either paid off but wasn't credited to your account, or debt you still owe.

Two other types of collections are evictions and tax liens (unpaid taxes). When you're developing, growing, or maintaining your credit, one of the worst things you can do is get evicted from a place of residence. Not only will it affect your credit score, it will also hurt when you attempt to apply for other places of residence or credit accounts. Once a lot of landlords see that you were previously addicted, they will often flip right past your application and move on to the next.

If you're going through financial hardships and you're having trouble finding employment, seek out some sort of housing or financial help even if it's government assistance. Do not let your status as a tenant get to the point of being evicted. It will be a task to overcome the addiction. Remember, it not only affects you short term, but also affects you long-term. Unless it is removed, an eviction can stay on your credit report for 7 years.

CHAPTER FIVE

Different types of Credit accounts

Installment loans

When it comes to your credit report with the 3 credit Bureaus Transunion, Equifax, and Experian, another form of accounts that will help your credit score out is installment loans. Installment loans are different from your credit card accounts. With your credit card accounts, you simply pay off the balance due every month and begin the next month as if you're starting from scratch. With installment loans, it takes a lot more patience than the patience practiced with credit card accounts; however the benefits of installment loans are worth it.

An installment loan is an amount of money that is repaid with interest over a certain period of time. Sometimes loans are 36 months, sometimes they're 48 months and sometimes they're 60 months. In some cases loans are much shorter than those terms. The different types of installment loans are mortgages, auto loans, personal loans, and student loans. Having one or more installment loans on your account help your credit score if you're making timely payments on your installment account. The reason installment loans help your credit report is because they provide your credit report with what I like to call a gumbo of accounts. You have a little bit of everything as far as accounts goes. You have your credit card account and then you have your installment accounts. Having a combination of both on your credit report helps your credit score, especially if all of your accounts are in good standing.

Earlier in the book I mentioned how signing up for an secured credit card will help your credit score out because it will help you develop credit. Another form of loan that will have a similar effect as the secured credit card is a secured loan.

Credit card accounts

Credit card accounts put a big dent in a large group of people's credit score. The average credit card account carries interest. When consulting clients with their credit, majority of them believed their credit card account wouldn't hurt their credit score as long as they were making the minimum payment on time every month. Some people have credit cards from department stores or other financial institutions. Credit cards are something you want to manage the right way because if not they can harm your score in a major way, as previously stated in an earlier chapter.

Secured loans

A secured loan is a loan through a bank that you fund in order to help establish or improve your credit score. Secured loans are usually intended for people who have bad or fair credit and need to improve their score to a level where they qualify for unsecured loans. The way the secured loan works is you find a financial institution and tell them you want to apply for a secured loan. They'll ask you to provide your payment as collateral, which will basically be the loan amount similar to the secured credit card I discussed in earlier chapters. They'll take your money and set up an installment plan for you to pay off the total loan amount. At the end of the loan term, you get your money back if you meet the banks requirements, similar to the secured credit card. Whatever you do, please do not be delinquent on a balance for your secured loan. You also will need to practice a great deal of patience and discipline during the full term of your loan. If you have extra funds available, you'll probably want to pay the secured loan off before the term is over with. Don't! Simply practice patience and pay the amount due each month. Paying the loan out full term month by month will help your credit more than paying the full loan off immediately or in a couple of months. Doing the latter can and probably will actually hurt your credit score.

Personal loans

Another form of an installment is a personal loan. A personal loan is much different from a secured loan. With a personal loan, you don't have to provide the bank with collateral money to fund your loan. The bank will determine your loan amount, interest rate, and term based on your credit history and credit score. There is a chance of you being declined of a personal loan if you're credit score is not high enough or having a lack of income on your behalf. As with secured loans, personal loans are to be paid over a term period. Make sure you're making your monthly payments on time for the length of your loan.

Student loans

Student loans are another form of installment loans. Make sure you're paying towards your student loans every month over their term period. Paying your student loan installment every month not only lowers the amount of debt you have on your credit report, it also improves your debt to credit ratio on your credit report. Of course, with student loans you don't have to pay off your full balance immediately. If you can afford to pay off your full loan balance without it placing you in a future financial bind, by all means do it. However, you risk the chance of your credit score dropping due to an installment loan being paid in full. I believe paying off student loan debt in full will benefit you more long-term than not paying it off when you have the funds to do so. Try your hardest not to miss any student loan payments, because it will have an effect on your credit report if you do.

Auto loans

Auto loans are probably the most common type of loan many people have experience with. Whether you have poor credit or excellent credit, most people have experience with auto loans. The tricky thing about auto loans unlike personal loans and mortgages is you can get an auto loan with poor credit or no credit. The trick comes in because, yes you'll qualify for an auto loan, but your interest rate will have you paying double the prices in triple the time for a car that may not life the whole term of the loan.

I once knew a woman who purchased a 7-year-old car from a "Buy Here, Pay Here" dealership. She had poor credit, and didn't have the money to purchase a vehicle out of pocket. She needed a car for transportation because she didn't live near any public transportation stops. The Buy here, Pay here dealership approved her of a loan for the car. They gave her an interest rate of 22%. Her payments for an old car were well above the price anyone with a fair or average credit score would be paying for a 7-year-old car. They also stretched her loan amount out to 72 months, which is a 6-year term.

Here's a quick word of advice from me to whoever is considering a 72-month auto loan. If you have to get a 72-month auto loan your credit is either poor or you cannot financially afford the vehicle you're attempting to purchase. Purchasing a vehicle you cannot afford will hurt your credit score eventually because it is almost inevitable you'll miss a payment or two over the term of your loan. So many financial mishaps can happen over the term of 6 years. You can lose a job, get sick, or even have a business that fails. The longer your installment loan such as an auto or personal loan, the more dangerous it becomes. The higher the interest rate also expands the risk of it take more time to pay your loan off in full in time. My advice to anyone reading this is to avoid 72-month auto loans, especially if they're attempting to develop, grow, or maintain credit. Vehicles depreciate fast, and you don't want to be still making payments on a vehicle that has lost most of its value before it's paid off.

Collection accounts and bankruptcies

If you have a large number of these two forms of accounts on your credit report, more than likely your credit score isn't doing too well. Collection and bankruptcy accounts are what I like to consider as throwaway accounts, meaning there are not many productive options when it comes to rectifying them. The best option is to not have any of your accounts reach the status of a collection account or bankruptcy. If you're already in that predicament for bankruptcy, the best option is to work on all other areas of your credit profile in order to at least consistently boost your score during the term of those accounts being in bad standing. Tax liens used to be reported, but in 2018 they were removed from accounts by the 3 major credit bureaus due to new changes to remove civil judgments and tax liens.

CHAPTER SIX

How to handle collections and avoid hard inquiries

Collections play a major role in your credit score. Through my experience with credit scoring, I've learned that collections can drop your score significantly depending on the number of collections you have on your credit report. One thing about collections is they normally stay on your account for 7 years. Unless you have some written agreement with a collections agency to remove an account in collections the collection account will still stay on your credit report for 7 years, even if you've paid off the balance of the collection in full.

If your collection account is more than 3 years old, I advise you to consider not paying off the collection account. There is a possibility the collection account has either changed agencies or changed the total balance amount by the 3rd year. I've witnessed this happen to myself and countless of other people over the years. Collection agencies buy and sell accounts that were placed in collections. Your collection account can potentially switch hands between 3 or more collection agencies over the span of the 7-year period that your account is in collections.

What I do advise in regards to collection accounts is disputing every single collection account on your credit report. If the collection is new, dispute it. If the collection is older, dispute it. The reason I'm advising you to dispute the collection accounts on your credit report is because the collection agency has to prove the collection debt belongs to you. If they don't prove to the credit bureaus that it is your debt within 30 days, then they have to delete it from your credit report. If they are able to prove the debt belongs to you then things still work in your favor because you'll at least know what you're up against when it comes to the amount of debt you have and the amount of collections you have. I always tell people disputing your collections is a 50/50 swing. It can go either way, so you don't lose anything by disputing the accounts. I'll touch more on how to dispute your collection account with the 3 credit bureaus later on in this book.

If you receive a letter after you disputed your collection account and it states the debt does belong to you, then you have two options. You can try to get in touch with the collection agency that currently owns your debt (collection account), and try to work out an arrangement where you can pay off an agreed upon balance and they promise in writing to remove it from the 3 credit bureaus in return. I did this once before and it worked. Or you can just choose to wait out your 7 year term period while working on other areas of your credit account. There is a possibility the debt will be removed from your credit report by the 3 credit bureaus prior to the 7th year of the collection account, and that's why I advise people to wait it out if the debt isn't removed as a result of disputes. There are ways to still improve your credit score even with collection accounts on your report. I had a couple of clients who lost disputes for a couple of accounts they had in collections, and they were still able to get in the good credit range because of their work in the other areas of credit such as on-time payments, number of accounts in good standing, and a small number of hard inquiries.

There are risks involved with contacting your collection agency. The age of your collection can be restarted if the collection agency can prove the debt is yours after speaking with you. I always advise my clients to not contact or speak with collection agencies. It's sort of like spilled milk. The collection is already on their credit report, and there's a high possibility it will remain on the credit report even after the debt has been paid to the collection agency.

Some people reading this may not have the patience to wait until collections accounts fall off their account, but I advise you to practice patience if your dispute letters fail. This book is all about a process. As with any process, a certain level of patience is required in order for the process to reach its full potential. Save the money you would use to pay off your collection, and instead use that money to pay down balances on your installment loans or outstanding balances if you have any. If you don't have any installment loans or outstanding balances, use the money you were planning on paying your collections off with and either invest it towards your secured credit card account if you have one, or simply save the money for future needs.

The best way to get a loan without receiving multiple hard inquiries

When I attempted to get a car during the time period when my credit score was bad, I went to multiple dealerships in search for a car. In total, I went to 4 different car dealerships over a two-month period and they all ran my credit report. In total, I ended up with 26 total inquiries on my Transunion credit report from the 4 different car dealerships. One of the reasons why checking all 3 of your credit reports is so important, is the total number of accounts or hard inquiries can differ between all 3 major credit reports. I only had 13 hard inquiries on my Equifax credit report, which was half of the 26 hard inquiries I had with Transunion. What made matters even worse was I didn't even get approved for a car loan. Actually, I did get approved for a car loan by Drive time, but I decided not to go with their offer because I felt like they were over-charging me for the car and their bi-weekly payment requirement didn't fit my financial situation at that time.

As I began to grow my credit score, I told myself that I would not allow myself to get high amounts of hard inquiries anymore in order to get approved for a loan. I came to the realization that the whole credit scoring system is sort of a game. You can either play the game, or sit back and get played. I knew those car dealerships were after a sale. They honestly don't care about the potential of hard inquiries hurting your credit score. Their job is to get a sale and get the most out of the sale. If that means a longer loan term and highest interest rate, they'll do it.

When car dealerships are trying to find you the best deal for your poor or fair credit situation, they're going to more than likely contact a handful of financial institutions. Depending on how poor your credit and financial situation is they will probably contact much more than a handful of financial institutions, sort of like they did in my situation with those high amount of hard inquiries. Honestly, the dealerships often times don't treat you well when they know there's a chance you may not get approved for a car loan. There's a night and day difference between the way they treat you when they know you're getting a car, and the way they treat you when they don't know if you'll get approved for a loan for the car.

Two years after being denied for a vehicle loan by the 4 car dealerships, my credit score rose to a 683 with Equifax. This was due to me putting in work and applying everything I've learned during the years regarding credit. The 26 hard inquiries with Transunion and 13 hard inquiries with Equifax were removed from my credit report by both bureaus because the two-year hard inquiry period expired. I was in the market for a new car. My current car had gotten to the point where I was tired of getting it repaired. Amazingly, the car had over 260,000 miles on it and I just got a new motor put in it a year or so prior. It was time to give the car up, but I also didn't have the money saved up for a reliable vehicle. At the time, most reliable vehicles in my market were selling for $5,000 minimum. I stress the word reliable, because at the time I had a job that required more driving than the average person does.

I knew I didn't want to get a high amount of hard inquiries while trying to get a vehicle, so I decided to go with my current bank. I'm not going to lie; I pondered over applying for the car loan for weeks. I went back and forth in my head about the pros and cons of applying with my bank. "What if I don't get approved?" I constantly thought. At the time, I didn't know what my FICO score was. I knew what my Credit Karma score was, however your Credit Karma score is your Vantage 3.0 score and most financial institutions such as my bank use FICO scores when determining lending.

One day I was home on my laptop and I decided to apply for the auto loan through my bank. I went to my bank's website and went to apply for an auto loan section. I filled out all of the necessary information, including the amount I would like for the auto loan. Within less than a minute I was approved for the loan amount I applied for. They gave me the option to choose the year terms that I wanted to pay off the loan in. I had the option to either pay off the auto loan in 3 years, 4 years, or 5 years. The 3-year auto loan provided the lowest interest rate of the 3-year terms, but I decided to go with the 5-year term, which was 60 months. The 60-month term came along with a 4.49% interest rate and I was happy about it compared to the interest rates I've seen other people getting approved for over the years.

One main benefit of being approved for the car loan through my bank was they only allowed me to purchase a vehicle with a select list of dealerships. The range of dealerships was wide so don't panic. The reason why the bank provides you with a list of dealerships that you can purchase your car from is because not only do they want to make sure the dealership is legit, they also want to protect you from purchasing a bad vehicle. The bank technically owns the vehicle until you pay off the loan, so it is understandable why they're cautious of where you purchase the vehicle. Based on the list, majority of the car dealerships listed were the major car dealerships in my city.

I printed out my loan paper and decided to go car shopping. A family friend told me allegedly car dealerships are not too pleased when you show up with a loan for a certain amount from your financial institution because they want to squeeze in their own fees and charges. I went to a total of three dealerships and my credit wasn't pulled once because of my loan paper. Of course, the dealerships wanted to run my credit. They told me they could get me a lower interest rate if I allowed them to pull my credit report. I vehemently denied the dealerships of pulling my credit report. I went to the last of the 3 dealerships and found the car I wanted and for a price that fit right into my loan amount. The dealership manager tried his hardest to get me to let them pull my credit report. Interesting story is he even told me that the hard pull wouldn't hurt my credit score. I debated him that pulling my credit report would definitely have a negative impact on my score. I knew he wasn't being honest because of those hard inquiries I received at the dealerships 2 years prior.

That's the problem that you have to solve. The dealerships and realtors will do anything to get a sale. I cannot say I disagree with their tactics because their job is to make sales. I do have an issue with the lack of morality that is often practiced against people who are not knowledgeable in the area of credit and personal finance. That is why it's so important for you to do as much research as possible before making an important purchase.

My advice to you is to try to get a loan from your personal bank or credit union before you try to get one anywhere else. Not only will it keep the amount of hard inquiries you receive down, you may also end up receiving the best loan term that fits you. Once your credit is in the 750 and above range, you can more than likely apply anywhere you desire for a loan and get approved. Until you reach that point, please use a personal bank or credit union as your first option. When shopping for a new house or car, the goal shouldn't only be making sure you receive the most favorable loan, it should also be making sure you keep the number of hard inquiries you receive down.

CHAPTER SEVEN

Develop, grow, and maintain your credit

Developing Credit
Range: Poor-Fair Credit

This chapter is going to be for people who are in the poor to fair credit score range. It doesn't matter if you're someone who doesn't have any credit history established or if you're someone with a lot of bad credit history established. If your credit is in the poor to fair range, it needs to be developed. Reading that may be a tough pill to swallow for some people, however there's beauty in starting from the bottom. Think of it as you're being presented to mold your credit score the way you want it to be molded. You're basically an architect working with foundation and you're going to build your credit as far as you put in the work to build your building (credit) as high as you want it to be. The developing credit stage is the blueprint for your credit portfolio for the rest of your life. It is very important for you to develop your credit before you grow and maintain your credit. You cannot complete the two steps of growing and maintaining your credit without first developing it. I'm going to go through the steps you need to complete during the credit development stage.

Reviewing your credit report

I want you to come into this tasks knowing your objective is not only to know what you have to dispute, but you also need to know the accounts you have and exactly how much debt you have for each account. Your mindset should be focused on paying off bad debt and maintaining your good debt. The first step with developing your credit is, knowing what is on your credit report. That means obtaining a copy of your credit report from each credit bureau, Transunion, Equifax, and Experian. You can either choose to purchase your credit report or you can get one free credit report annually through annualcreditreport.com. Once you obtain your credit report, review each credit report from each bureau one at a time. Do not assume the information listed on one bureau's credit report will be listed on the other bureau's credit report as well. Sometimes certain items such as hard inquiries and collections aren't added by all of the bureaus. Transunion can have 13 hard inquiries listed, whereas Equifax has 28, and Experian only has 3. Be very observant when reviewing each one of your 3 credit reports.

With a writing utensil and notepad handy, notate the things I suggest you notate when reviewing your credit report. There are very important things you should look for when reviewing your credit score. The first thing you want to look for is all of your personal information such as your name, address, past address, as well as place of employment if you have one. You want to make sure all of that information is spelled right and listed right. After that you want to make sure all of the accounts listed are accounts that belong to you. This includes active accounts, collections, delinquencies, student loans, vehicle loans, personal loans, hard inquiries, as well as any bankruptcies. If you do find an error in your name or any of the previous mentioned information, make sure you dispute those things. I'll speak more on how to dispute later in this book.

The next thing you want to look for is any accounts that are currently in collections. If you find any accounts that are in collections, make sure you notate them one by one in your notebook. Even if you feel like these accounts are past accounts that belong to you, you should still dispute collection accounts to the 3 credit bureaus. The reason is because collection agencies have to prove to the bureaus that the collection account belongs to you. The 3 bureaus give the collection agencies 30 days to show proof that the account in collection is your debt, and if they don't provide proof, by law the bureaus are supposed to remove the account. Sometimes you do a dispute and the collection agency is able to prove the debt belongs to you. If they are able to prove it's your debt you have two options. You can either pay off the debt on the account that's in collections or you can wait until the collection account falls off your credit report. I strongly suggest you take the advice of the latter. Contacting a collection agency in reference to an account in collection has potential to start a big fire that you may not being willing to put out. Also, something to keep in mind is even if you do pay off a collection account, there's a chance that the account will still stay on your credit report if the collection agency doesn't request that it gets removed by the bureaus. Normally collection accounts stay on your credit 7 years before they're removed. I've saw plenty of instances where the credit bureaus removed collection accounts prior to 7 years being up. This is where practicing patience comes into play, especially if the collection accounts are still on your report after you've disputed them.

The next thing I want you to look for your hard inquiries. Unlike your collection accounts, you're not going to dispute your hard inquiries unless they don't belong to you. Typically, hard inquiries stay on your credit report for two years. They usually have a harder impact on your credit report during the first year, and while it still affects your score after the first year, it doesn't have nearly as much of an impact as it did in year one. Keep in mind; the whole idea behind this book is for you to take hold of mastering your credit portfolio. Notate each hard inquiry that you have as well as the date when they were first listed on your report. The date the hard inquiry was first listed will let you know a time frame of when the hard inquiry will be removed from your credit report by the credit bureaus. Remember, they stay on your account for two years. The word patience keeps being preached for a reason. It is very important for you to practice patience during the two-year period when your hard inquiries are on your report.

The next thing you should look for on your credit report is all of your active accounts. This includes current credit card accounts if you have any, student loans, personal loans, bankruptcies, auto loans, and any other account you may have on your report. Your task is to find a way to pay all of your delinquent accounts and get them up to date. This is the part of developing your credit where sacrifice comes into play. You're going to have to cancel some extracurricular expenses you may have going towards other things in order to complete this task. Whatever you currently purchase in excess, whether its clothes, eating out often, trips, or whatever it may be, you're going to have to put those things to the side until all of your accounts are up to date. You may even have to pick up a part time gig or side hustle to help you during this time, but whatever it takes make sure you get all of your accounts on your credit report up to date. Does this mean pay off all of your accounts in full?

No. I don't expect people to pay off their auto, personal, or student loans immediately. However, I expect for you to at least get those accounts up to date to the current month's payment if those accounts are behind. I also recommend you pay down your credit card debt to zero if you have any. If your credit card is reporting as late every month or constantly being charged interest, you are not managing your credit cards the way someone who's trying to develop good or excellent credit should be managing them.

The number one goal during the credit development stage is to get current. Once you get to the point where you are current on all of your accounts listed on your credit report, then you can go to the next step. Enhancing your credit is what leads up to growing your credit. It is very important for you to enhance your credit portfolio. Enhancing your portfolio simply means adding one or more new accounts to your credit portfolio. This will help you with your foundation of the building I was referring to earlier in this chapter.

3 ways to enhance your credit

For poor and fair credit

When you have poor or fair credit, you don't really have many options as far as financial institutions willing to take a chance on you. You either don't have enough of a credit history established, or you do have credit history established but its bad history. Either way, you have to find a way to establish a good relationship with financial institutions. How do you establish a good relationship with them? We talked about this earlier in the book with the girl selling snacks. You have to prove to

STRATEGIES TO MASTER CREDIT

the financial lenders that you have the ability to pay them back in a timely fashion. Your ability to pay financial lenders back establishes and builds a rapport with them, and after that they're willing to extend more lines of credit to you. And it's so interesting because financial lenders view lending candidates similarly. If one lender sees you doing well with another financial institution and establishing a good rapport through on time payments, they're going to want to extend offers to you as well.

Apply for a Secured Credit Card

One way to enhance your credit is by applying for a secured credit card. Earlier in the book I discussed secured credit cards and how they can help you out when you have poor or fair credit. I won't personally refer you to any secured credit card companies since they're not paying me, but I will say before you decide to apply for a secured credit card, please be sure to read reviews regarding them. Google is your best friend when it comes to finding the best financial institutions to get a secured credit card from. Your personal bank if you do have one is usually a good first place to start your inquiries.

Apply for a Secured Personal Loan

The second way to enhance your credit is by applying for a secured personal loan. I also explained the process of applying for a secured loan earlier in this book. A secured loan helps in terms of the type of account in your credit portfolio. Whatever you do, please do not miss payments when paying on your secured loan.

Auto Loan

The third way to enhance your credit is an auto loan. I highly recommend you follow one of the first two ways to enhance your credit before going out and picking up an auto loan. My reasoning for suggesting you use one of the previous two options is because they're the safer options for your credit portfolio. You have poor or fair credit, so applying for an auto loan would mean you're going to have an interest rate that's high, no matter how much money you put down. You'll be paying more money than you should for a vehicle if you do decide to apply for an auto loan with poor or fair credit. Unless you desperately need a vehicle and don't have the money to purchase one in full, I would suggest sticking to the first two options of enhancing credit.

No matter which option you choose, it is very important for you to make all of your monthly payments on time. If your option is the secured credit card, make sure you keep in mind the utilization. Be sure to keep your utilization under 10% of your credit limit. If your option is the secured personal loan, make sure you're making your monthly payments in a timely manner. If you choose the option of purchasing a vehicle, please be sure to not have any late payments. You will only harm your credit by having late payments. Whichever option you choose: do not apply for any new lines of credit once your secured credit card or loan. You should wait a minimum of one full year before apply for any new credit accounts. If you have a secured card, wait until your card graduates to an unsecured card before applying for new accounts.

During the credit development stage you want to make sure you're not score watching. Watching your score will discourage you because you may not see the big jump that you may be looking for in your score. If you want a credit score of 700+, you have to practice patience as well as complete the necessary steps to developing your credit. Your mission is bigger than score watching. Remember, you're in the foundation stage. Do you think an architect gets discouraged in the foundation laying stage when they see a building not up yet? If they did, chances are the project would either get delayed or won't happen at all. The same applies to developing your credit. Practice patience, stay disciplined, make sacrifices, and you'll be ready for the next stage which is growing your credit.

Growing your credit
Range: Fair credit

If a financial lender asks someone what's their credit score and their response is, "It's alright." There's a big chance that person is in the fair credit range. That's completely fine because the average person is in this credit range. The interesting thing about this credit range is there's room for improvement. I have come across many people who have fair credit and they believe their credit is good enough. Some of them believe their credit can't be better and some are satisfied with where it currently stands.

I'm assuming if you're in this credit range you have at least some credit accounts established. You more than likely have at least one credit card or some type of loan. When I was in this credit range I was happy, because I was able to get just about any loan I applied for. However, I wasn't satisfied with being in this range because I knew I wanted the best rates possible, and the only way to get the best rates possible is to have excellent credit. Sometimes I hear stories about people being happy with a 590 credit score because it puts them above the 580 credit score range to get a home loan. There are also people in the 620 score range who are fine with their score for the same reason.

Now, I didn't decide to write this book to scold the readers. The purpose of writing this book is to educate and inform you about credit. If you're satisfied with a 580 or 620 credit score because it helps you get approved for a home loan, you should re-think the true purpose of credit. If you are approved for a home loan with a credit score of 580 or 620, you're not going to get the best interest rate possible. In fact, you're probably going to get the worst rate possible depending on the lender. That's a major issue when you factor in the average home loan being for 30 years. That's 30 years of high interest. There's so many things that can take place during those 30 years which can make your high interest rate a heavy burden and may even put you in danger of losing your home. Every home loan is not fixed rate loan, and a lot of people also don't factor in the potential rise in property value due to annual property assessment in some States. That's another book, but I believe purchasing a home is a luxury, not a necessity. I don't feel like purchasing a home is something you have to do immediately, especially before you establish good or excellent credit. There are always the options of leasing or renting before purchasing a home. Some people may think it's more of a financial burden to lease or rent a home instead of buying, but it goes back to the temporary sacrifices that will have to be made while attempting to establish good or excellent credit.

If you are in the fair to good credit range and already have a home loan that you're currently paying on, you can use your home loan account to your advantage to better your credit score. Make sure all of your monthly payments are made on time. I don't know the financial status of each person reading this book, but if you can afford to and your financial lender allows you to, double up on payments in order to give yourself a cushion on your home loan. Being current on your home loan and making all of your payments on-time without late fees will not only lower your overall balance on your credit report; it will also help with your payment history.

Unlike the poor to fair credit range, if you apply for an auto loan it will more than likely help your credit score. In this range, you may not get the best interest rate possible but there's a chance that you can get a decent interest depending on the current interest rate market by financial lenders. The first couple of months after receiving an auto or personal loan expect to see your credit score take a dive. It can be 5 to 10 points, or it can be much more than 10 points. No matter how many points your score lowers, do not panic. It will go up after a couple of months of good payments. In 6 months to a year, your credit score will more than likely be higher than the score you had when you initially applied for your auto or personal loan.

If you're in this range you have the leverage to apply for new credit accounts. At this stage in your credit portfolio, having different types of accounts will actually help your credit in the long run as long as your accounts are in good standing. You have the credit score to at least get approved for an unsecured credit card. My method is to apply for a credit card that has no annual fee. This will keep you away from the burden of having to make annual fee payments in order to keep your account open.

Growing your credit score is simply figuring out what works best for your current credit profile. If you have a credit report that's full of student loans, it probably won't do your credit score any justice by going out and getting another student loan. If you have a lot of credit card accounts, the best option may be getting a different kind of account such as an installment account. If your accounts are auto and home loan, adding a credit card can help in terms of having an extra account that's not the same type of account as your loans.

Some people may be reading this book and think I'm encouraging people to get into deeper debt than they currently are. I'm not. The advice I'm giving for this credit range is for people who are capable of making on-time payments and financially capable of opening up new lines of credit. If you're in a financial bind or struggling financially, you can still grow your credit by simply getting your accounts balances to up to date and paying your open accounts on-time. You don't have to be wealthy or have extra cash floating around in order to grow your credit score. Growing your credit score will eventually lead you to a score that you desire to maintain.

Maintaining your credit
Range: Good-Excellent credit

This is the final stage for your credit profile. This is the stage where you want to be. This is the stage where you basically are on cruise control. If you're in the good to excellent credit range, I expect you to already know how to manage debt. In fact, you will not get to this credit range if you don't know how to manage your debt, unless you're a debt free person who has multiple good and long-standing accounts that you're listed as an authorized user on. There's no independence in that. Having excellent credit is like being on the priority list when it comes to financial institution. If you ever flew on an airplane, when the plane is boarding they call the priority boarders to board the plane before the people who aren't on the priority list. When you have excellent credit, financial institutions want to do business with you. They want to give you the home loan. They want to give you the auto loan. They want you to sign up for their credit cards. In fact, when you have excellent credit the financial institutions want you to apply for their premium credit cards.

When you have excellent credit, your goal should always be preserving and maintaining your excellent credit. I listed good credit as the range because you transition from good credit to excellent credit. You have so many options once you reach good credit to excellent credit range. Yes, you can expect your score to fluctuate but it will continue to be in the good to excellent range if you continue to do the things you did that led you up to this point.

One trick I've learned while having excellent credit is sometimes, you'll come across the threat of your score leaving the excellent credit range. Let's say you have a home loan or auto loan that's close to being paid off. Once you finally pay off the loan in full, the account will disappear from your credit report and will hurt your score as a result. This is due to you having one less credit account. Depending on where your score is in the excellent range, it can lead to your score dropping less than a 760. To counter it, you can either open up another installment loan or credit card. This isn't something you have to do, because having a score that's as high as this range provides, your credit is pretty much in a good place. Credit is subjective depending on what's on your credit report, and only you know what will help or hurt your credit score.

One thing you can do when in the excellent credit range is use your credit as leverage for the future, such as using your credit to invest in real estate or your business. You can add your kids or loved ones to your credit card accounts as authorized users. The idea is to add them to your longest and most established credit card account that's in good standing. This will in return improve their credit score because the credit card account will be added to their credit report in the same good standing that you have it in, with the same lengthy credit history.

When you're in the good and excellent credit range I advise you to be conscious of your hard inquiries. You have credit that's in good standing, so it's not hard to be tempted by offers for rewards credit cards, personal loans, and other forms of loans because you know your chances of being approved with a good interest rate are just about automatic. However, that doesn't mean you should apply for new credit with every opportunity that is presented to you. By doing so, it can and more than likely will affect your credit score negatively. Be conscious of where and what credit accounts you apply for and be sure to keep your number of new accounts at a manageable level and hard inquiries low. If you somehow have a slip up and your credit begins to take a large dip, refer back to the sections previous sections for poor and fair credit. Applying that information will get you right back on track when paired with consistency.

CHAPTER EIGHT

Important tools

How to dispute accounts on your credit report

Disputing accounts on your credit report is very important in the credit building process. Your credit report is basically your financial resume. When you send your employment resume to potential employers, the potential employer browses over your information to review your credentials and see if you're the best fit for their company. A similar process happens when financial institutions review your credit report. They're checking to see if you qualify for a loan with their institution, and if you do qualify, they want to know your previous financial history so they could determine if you're capable of making the payments on the loan.

Even if you believe the information on your credit report is correct, you should still dispute your credit report in order to make sure the 3 bureaus verify the correct information. Please make sure you pay attention in detail to every section of your credit report. Make sure all of your personal information listed is correct as well as the creditors or financial lenders information is correct. One thing to keep in mind is your collection accounts are supposed to be removed 7 years from the first day of delinquency. Your bankruptcies are supposed to be removed from your credit report 7 years from the filing date of the bankruptcy for Chapter 13, and 10 years from the filing date of the bankruptcy for Chapter 7. If any of those types of accounts remain on your credit report after the listed time period, please make sure to list those accounts in your dispute letter.

A big mistake some people make is not disputing their credit report. I view it as leaving free money on the table because you never know what negative accounts you can have removed from your credit report based on the collection agencies not being able to verify the information. It's taking a swing at a pitch for majority of the time less than $30 American dollars.

By law, the federal Fair Credit Reporting Act (FCRA) protects you when it comes to making sure all of the information on your credit report is accurate. The FCRA law was passed in 1970 in order to ensure the information on credit reports is being reported as accurate. It also insures the privacy of personal information. The FCRA governs how the 3 major credit bureaus can collect and share your information. By law, you're entitled to one free credit report from each of the 3 major credit bureaus. There are websites where you can use to get a free credit report. Simply Google 'free annual credit report' and pick the company of your liking.

When disputing your credit report under the FCRA, the reporting agencies have 30 days to verify that your account(s) are accurate. If they're able to verify the debt belongs to you, the reporting agency has 30 days to make sure any wrong information on the account is corrected. If they cannot verify the account belongs to the borrower, the reporting agency has 30 days before they must delete the account from the borrower's credit report. This is an area where a lot of people win credit report disputes because a lot of collection agencies cannot verify the debt belongs to the disputing person. The collection agency is more than likely not the original company who owned the debt. Collection agencies often purchase debt for cheap from the original lender in order to see if they can work a deal out with a borrower in order to pay off debt. From the collection agency's standpoint, it's a win-win situation since they purchased the debt for cheap and the payoff can sometimes be hundreds or thousands of dollars.

Send your dispute letters through the postal service

The most effective way to file a credit report dispute is through mail. There are risks involved because of identity theft, however when you file a dispute on the Internet, you risk the chance of losing the dispute. Online disputes are done through an encrypted connection. Sure, it's quicker, but I believe mailing your dispute letter is the best option. When you mail your dispute letters, the bureau's employees read and verify your information. They will also send confirmation stating your information was received and verified. When you dispute through mail, it lets you know an actual person and not a computer program reviewed your dispute information.

Things that should be included in your mail package

When mailing your disputes you want to make sure you have all of the information from your credit report that you want to dispute. Each of the 3 major credit bureaus has their own credit report, so you need to send a dispute letter to each credit bureau separately. That means you should have a separate letter sent to Experian, Equifax, and Transunion.

First, you want to verify the mailing address for disputes for each of the 3 credit bureaus. This can be done by either contacting the credit bureaus by phone, online, or doing a quick Google search of each credit bureau's mailing address for disputes. Include the credit bureaus name and specific mailing address in the top left corner of your letter.

You also want to include a copy of your personal ID (license or passport), as well as a copy of your social security number. This is to verify that you're disputing your actual information. You also want to make sure you list your social security number, home mailing address, as well as your name of course. Please provide paper copies of your social security number as well as your personal identification such as your license.

You may want to send your letters priority as well. I did have one situation occur when I sent a dispute letter first class and it took the bureau longer than a week for the credit bureau to receive my dispute letter. Of course, wondering where my letter was, I inquired and spoke to the customer service rep where the letter was currently being held, and the postal employee informed me the postal service allegedly place first class mail behind priority mail. I cannot verify the accuracy or truth to that, so I would say send the mail whichever way you believe will result in your letters getting to the credit bureaus the fastest. Just make sure your letters are sent certified with a return receipt requested. Please give the credit bureaus at least 30 days to respond to your request.

Below is a sample of a dispute letter. Keep in mind; this is not an actual dispute letter, however, it is showing you how your dispute letter should look. Another thing to keep in mind when writing your letters is your credit report won't show the full account number on your listed accounts. Do not be alarmed when you see an account number that looks similar to 47284***. Just copy the name of the account and numbers listed for the account number in detail, followed by the marks and the bureaus will know which account numbers you're referring to.

Mark Tylerwinkle
3738 Blah Blah Ave
Dreamland, AZ 71493
SSN: 000-00-0000
Birthdate: 3/3/1988

Experian
0000 Address St,
Gummy worms, NJ 74783

I am disputing the accounts listed below. According to the Fair Credit Reporting ACT (FCRA), 15 U.S.C. 1681, you are required by Federal Law to review and verify the below listed account information is accurate. I am requesting you to please verify the accounts listed below. Please provide correspondence with physical verifiable proof regarding the accounts listed below.

State farm – account # 2838****   9/4/2013
Sprint- account # 382*****   3/17/2012
Primary basket bank- account # 38472***   11/23/2015

I am requesting you remove all unverified accounts from my credit report immediately, according to the FCRA.

Sincerely,
Mark Tylerwinkle

Always keep an eye on your credit report

Once you have went through and applied all of the information provided in this book, you're more than likely sitting with a credit score higher than the one you had when you first began reading this book. You now know how to develop, grow, and maintain your credit profile. You have all of the information needed in order to continue to improve your credit profile and increase your credit score.

It is important for you to stay up to date with your credit report. Identity theft is big these days, especially with people having so much access to people's personal information due to the Internet. There are tools that can be used to protect you and some of those tools are even free of charge. There are websites that provide you with a free credit report. Websites such as Credit Karma provide free access to your credit report.

In reference to Credit Karma, people tend to use the website to keep up with their credit score. I tell the people I consult with not to use Credit Karma as a credit score indicator, but instead use Credit Karma as a weekly credit report update. Credit Karma and other free websites provide you with the ability to monitor your score weekly, and if not weekly at least monthly. If you do have a credit card account, your financial institution will usually provide you with monthly access to your credit report and sometimes your score from one of the 3 major bureaus.

Credit Karma monitors your credit report from both Equifax and Transunion every 7 days. This will come in handy if a new unexpected account shows up on your report or if someone is using your identity for illegal practices. I always tell people I consult to try to log-in to Credit Karma every 7 days to stay up to date with their report, and if they can't log in every 7 days, at least log in once a month.

Reviewing your credit report every month allows you to stay up to date on your overall balance, your debt to credit ratio, your hard inquiries, as well as your payment history on your accounts. It's a great tool to make month-to-month adjustments that can impact your credit profile and score in a positive way. Take advantage of all of the free websites and tools that provide you with a free credit report.

In closing

I hope that you've concluded reading this book with the great feeling of confidence that you can turn your credit profile around positively. I did it, and plenty of other people with worst credit profiles than the one I had did it as well. Good and excellent credit is not something that requires you to be a scholar in order to achieve. You simply have to combine applying what you've learned with effort, and patience. One of my main goals in life is to help and uplift other people. For me, there was no fun in keeping the knowledge in this book to myself. You can always refer back to this information at any point in your life and refresh your knowledge on credit.

I ask that after you're done reading, you share the information or book with someone who may be in need of it. It doesn't matter if that person is an adult or if they are a child who wants to learn about personal finances and credit. I don't believe public schools teach credit as a subject. Introducing a child early to knowledge concerning credit has a great chance of benefiting them once they become young adults.

I hope you apply all that you've learned and the information benefits you in a way that betters the lives of yourself and your loved ones. In my personal opinion, understanding credit isn't as complex as it seems. The one main factor to turning your credit profile around for the better is your own effort. I truly hope your effort made towards improving your credit profile matches the knowledge you've gained from reading this book. I hope I provided everyone reading with at least an important nugget to get over the hump of credit issues. Remember, patience and consistency are the keys.